URBAN L

Published by Arcturus Publishing Limited
26/27 Bickels Yard, 151–153 Bermondsey Street
London SE1 3HA

This edition printed in 2006

Printed in China

ISBN 1-84193-364-3

URBAN LEGENDS

They say that truth is often stranger than fiction, and so it would appear when browsing through this collection of urban myths and incredible stories. Of course, whether these tales are really true can never be proven, as they have now passed into folklore, added to and embellished with each re-telling.

We leave it to you decide which stories in this compendium ring true and which are too off-the-wall to be believable. What we can guarantee is that you won't be bored with our selection, which includes loony lawsuits, crazy criminal misdemeanours, humiliating mistakes and mind-boggling misfortunes. Some of these tales will send a chill down your spine while others will have you laughing in amazement at the sheer stupidity of your fellow citizens of the world.

True or false, these are stories you will want to tell your friends about.

Bus driver Michael Pemberton was driving 20 patients from an inner city psychiatric hospital to an institution in the countryside. As the patients were sedated, Michael thought it would be all right to stop at a roadside caff for a break. However, to his horror, he returned to find that every single one of the patients had escaped and the bus was now empty.

COMMITTED WORKER

Rather than admit to his mistake, Michael decided to cover up what had happened and drove round the city, picking up people from bus-stops along the way until he had 20 people in the bus. He then drove out to the countryside institution and told them that he was delivering the inner city patients. He also warned the staff that the patients were "highly excitable". When the case later came to court, a jury heard that it took eight hours before the 'patients' managed to convince the institution staff of Michael's cover-up.

SURPRISE VISITOR

Shelly Watson was about to step out of the shower when she realised that there were no clean towels in the bathroom.

Not worried, she walked naked downstairs to get some towels from the tumble drier, which was located on her back porch. She had not yet taken them out of the machine when she heard the milkman coming up the porch steps.

As he left the milk on the back step, Shelly quickly stepped inside a cupboard, in case he should look through the screen door and see her. As she stood waiting for him to leave, the cupboard door was suddenly flung open.

Standing in front of Shelly was the gas meter reader.

In her embarrassment she quickly blurted out, "Oh! I thought you were the milkman". Shelly's hubby, who had shown the meter reader where to find the meter, was not amused.

QUITE A SHOCK

When Eleanor Goodman walked in the kitchen and saw her husband Claude shaking violently with a wire running from his waist, seemingly towards the kettle, she immediately thought the worst, that he was being electrocuted.

She panicked and picked up a large piece of wood from near the back door, then brought the plank down heavily on to his arm, intending to jolt him away from the deadly current. She succeeded in breaking his arm in two places. Until then he had been happily dancing to the music on his Walkman and making a cup of tea.

Shaun Lewitt and former girlfriend Sadie Thomas' relationship had ended badly, and in May 2000 she had been forced to take out a restraining order.

Shaun decided that he was going to disobey the order and, since he knew Sadie would not let him into her Texas home through the front door, he decided to enter through the chimney. Rather predictably, the chimney was not wide enough to allow him to pass through. However, he managed to get quite a way down before realising he was stuck.

STUCK ON YOU

After a few hours, neighbours followed his cries, and firefighters were forced to knock down part of the chimney in order to get him out. Shaun was arrested on suspicion of burglary and stalking, while Sadie returned from her holiday in the Bahamas to find her chimney destroyed and her former boyfriend behind bars. She moved house shortly after.

A court case almost certain to fail was that of Indiana resident Shaun Perkins, who was struck by lightning while in the car park of the King's Island theme park in Mason, Ohio.

FINDING BLAME

Rather than feel grateful that he survived such an event with relatively minor injuries, Perkins chose instead to place the blame on the theme park's owners. His lawyer dismissed the usual idea that lightning is an act of God, saying: "That would be a lot of people's knee jerk reaction in these types of situations." Instead, he claimed it was the theme park's fault for not warning people that being outside in a thunderstorm was dangerous.

Asking for unspecified damages, Perkins was awarded exactly nothing.

JAILBREAK

Wabash Valley Correctional Facility in Indiana saw the attempted escape from prison of Jimmy Torin, who was serving time for fraud. His attempt failed for several reasons.

Jimmy arranged with two of his fellow prisoners to be smuggled out of the prison when the rubbish was collected and taken away. These two inmates were on garbage duty, and rather gleefully agreed to add a rubbish bag containing Jimmy to the other bags to be taken away. Pleased with his plan, Jimmy thought his freedom was just a few hours away. However, two hours later he was in the prison hospital, lucky to be alive. Jimmy's first mistake was to think that a human being could survive being tied up inside a plastic bag for hours. His second, and potentially fatal, mistake was to trust his life to two men who were serving time for murder. The third mistake was not to notice that all rubbish from the prison went through a trash compactor, to prevent people from escaping that way. Fortunately one of the binmen noticed that one bag was too heavy, and opened it to find Jimmy passed out inside.

UNLUCKY IN LIFE

August 1, 1999 was not a good night for Brendan Myner.

The 22-year-old broke into a house in Los Angeles at 3am with the intention of helping himself to the family's possessions, after being told they were on holiday. He was startled to discover the homeowner was not only home and wide awake, but was an armed police officer who had just got home from a shift. Officer Vargas fired wide to startle Myner, whose attempt to flee was then hampered by a fall into a cactus bed, followed by a trip over a wrought-iron fence that speared him in the groin. He managed to limp away and escape, but was arrested when he checked into the hospital for treatment for his injuries. The final straw was to discover that he had broken into the wrong house – the vacationing family lived next-door.

UNWANTED FAME

Daniel Clarkson of Canterbury, UK, suffered several instances of acute embarrassment after a drunken evening went horribly wrong.

Driving home slightly intoxicated after an evening in the pub, he should not have been surprised when he was pulled over after a policeman saw his car weaving all over the road. Desperate not to lose his licence, in the back of the patrol car, Daniel tore off his underwear and stuffed the fabric in his mouth, believing that it would soak up the alcohol. Needless to say, it did not. However, when he was in court, there was a class of law students who found Daniel's actions so funny they had to be removed from the courtroom. And, to add just one more embarrassment, his picture and story were then reported in the local newspaper. Said Daniel: "I will never drive drunk again."

NAME THAT TUNE

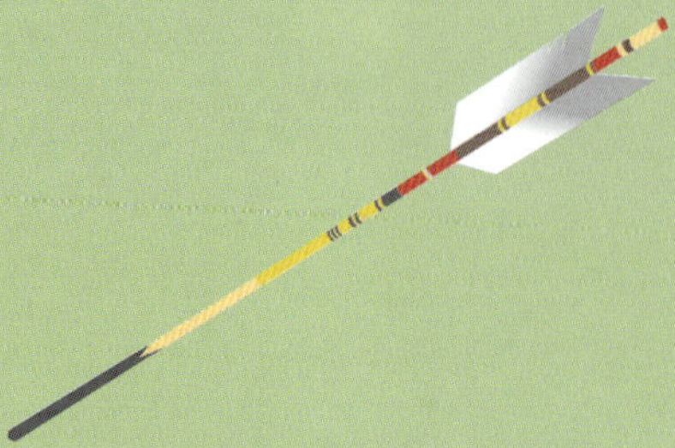

When Paul Tracy and Anna Yates were planning their wedding in 2001, they decided that it would be wonderfully romantic to walk down the aisle to 'their' song, 'Everything I do (I do it for you)' by Bryan Adams, the theme song from the film 'Robin Hood – Prince of Thieves', which they had seen on their first date.

They informed the organist of their decision and were delighted when 67-year-old Rose Moore confirmed that she was familiar with the song and would play it for them. She double-checked that they were sure, that they didn't want the traditional wedding march, and Paul assured her they had made their decision. Her reasons for double-checking became clear, however, on the big day, when Anna was forced to walk down the aisle to the strains of 'Robin Hood, Robin Hood, riding through the glen', the theme tune to the Sixties television show. Seems Rose wasn't a big Bryan Adams fan.

UNEXPECTED NEWS

Phillipe Trevous was so worried that a drugs test would reveal his secret, that he had cheated, he decided on a mastermind cover-up.

Cyclist Phillipe was taking performance-enhancing drugs in the hope of being selected for the French Olympic team, however a random drugs test panicked him into hiding a bottle of his girlfriend's urine in his shorts. All seemed to go smoothly, with the testers not noticing his ruse. Feeling rather smug, Phillipe's relief was to be short lived. Shortly after taking the test he received a phone call. The good news was that the test was negative for any illegal or banned substances. The bad news was the test was positive for pregnancy!

CRIME PAYS

Juvenile delinquent Carl Truman of Los Angeles won a staggering $74,000 plus medical expenses when he sued his neighbour, Noel Brown.

At first it seemed Truman had good reason for slapping Brown with a lawsuit, after all, Brown had run over Truman's hand with his car, a Honda Accord, breaking almost all the bones and rendering him – as Truman's lawyer phrased it – unable to work. However, Truman's 'job' was petty theft. The reason Brown had crushed Truman's hand in such a heartless manner, was that he had not seen the 17-year-old trying to steal his hubcaps when he started the car.

TROUBLE IN-LAW

Josephine Boone and John Kemp were married in 1997 in Glasgow, Scotland, in a lavish ceremony paid for by the bride's father, Graham.

In Graham's jacket pocket was a large roll of notes for paying the band, caterers etc. However, after leaving his jacket on the back of the chair while dancing, he returned to find that the money was missing. Broken-hearted that a friend or family member would do such a thing, Graham was forced to write cheques to cover the cost. A few weeks later, the Boone and Kemp families gathered together to watch the video of the ceremony and reception party. At one point during the film, the groom's father can be seen stealing the money from Graham's pocket! Josephine and John are still married, but there are no more joint family gatherings!

DO OR DIE

Peter Whitehead was determined to end his own life and decided to leave nothing to chance. Standing on the edge of a cliff, he tied a noose around his neck and secured the rope to a rock. He then drank poison and set his clothes on fire. As a final measure he decided to jump and shoot himself in the head.

However, the shot missed his head and cut through the rope. As a result, he plunged into the sea below, putting out the flames and causing him to vomit up the poison.

He was later rescued by a fisherman, but died of hypothermia on the way to the hospital.

An innocent gust of wind caused quite a few problems outside a dental surgery, and led to four people being admitted to hospital – Carl with whiplash, David with torn gum tissue, Sandra with two fingers missing and Maria with a head wound.

FLASH BANG WALLOP

It all started when Maria was about to enter the dentist surgery. A gust of wind lifted her skirt over her head, displaying her underwear to those driving past.

One of those drivers was Carl, who was so taken with the sight that he lost control of his car, which then veered off the road and into the dental surgery, where David was having his gums cleaned by Sandra. When the car came through the wall, David bit down in shock, cutting his gums and severing two of Sandra's fingers.

Maria was not to escape unharmed either, after watching events unfold, she was then struck by masonry falling after the collision.

MANNERS COST NOTHING

Multi-millionaire John Barrier had made his fortune buying and refurbishing buildings himself, and so was dressed in suitably scruffy clothes when he went to a bank in Spokane, Washington, to cash a cheque and get his parking ticket validated. The cashier took one look at his clothes and refused to validate the ticket.

She said that tickets were only validated after a transaction, and that cashing a cheque didn't count. Annoyed, Barrier told the cashier that he would, therefore, like to withdraw all his money from the bank and close his account. He then took his millions to a rival bank.

When asked about his decision to move banks, he replied: "If you have $1 in a bank or $1 million, I think they owe you the courtesy of stamping your parking ticket."

ALL-OVER TAN

Joan Sheldon's vacation was going well, for the first three days she sunbathed on the roof of her hotel almost all day, wearing a selection of skimpy bikinis.

Pleased with her tan, she was not happy, however, with the tan lines she was getting. The next day, on the roof, she decided to sunbathe in the nude, reasoning that no one could possibly see her so high up.

When she heard footsteps on the stairs she rolled over on to her front and pulled her towel over her bottom. A flustered man appeared, the assistant manager of the hotel.

He politely requested that Miss Sheldon put her bikini back on. A surprised Joan asked why.

– "What difference does it make?" she asked. "No one can see me up here."

– "Not exactly," said the assistant manager, blushing scarlet. "You are actually lying on the dining room skylight."

MISPLACED GENIUS

Cole Bartiromo, from Mission Viejo, California, had made more than $1 million on the stock market before his 18th birthday.

Sadly his methods were not legal, and the federal authorities accused him of fraud and ordered him to pay the money back. The case resulted in him being kicked off his high school baseball team, where he had been a keen player.

Bartiromo then filed a suit against his high school. His case was that he had been planning on a career as a professional baseball player, however talent scouts would now never discover him, as the school was not allowing him to play. He demanded that the school reimburse the salary that he had therefore 'lost' – i.e. the $50 million. The case is still pending.

CASH BONUS

35-year-old North Carolina resident Sol Vedejas was not the brightest man in the world, and never really made any money so his mother – whom he still lived with – was shocked to find $10,000 in his bag.

When she asked him how it got there she was even more surprised. Apparently Sol had gone to the bank on a cold November morning to take out $10 to go to the cinema. As it was a cold day he wore a ski mask, something that he did not remove when he entered the bank. When he handed the teller the slip with $10 written on it, the poor girl panicked and handed over the rather larger sum of $10,000. Slightly bemused, Sol then went to the cinema, thus eluding the police who were searching for him, and then went home. The money was returned and, as Sol had committed no crime, he was freed after police questioning.

FROM BEYOND THE GRAVE

Gene Rickman was horrified the day his dog Patches walked into the kitchen with a dead rabbit hanging from his mouth.

The rabbit belonged to his neighbour Simon Hopley's young daughter Alice. Other than being very dirty, Gene could find no signs of injury or blood on the rabbit and concluded that Patches must have broken the creature's neck. Determined that his dog should not be blamed, Gene shampooed and dried the dead rabbit, and replaced it in its cage, so Simon and Alice would assume it had died of natural causes. After a few days Gene bumped into Simon, who mentioned finding 'Snowy' dead in his cage. Gene commiserated until Simon said: "The strange thing was, he had died the day before and we had buried him in the garden. Someone had dug him up, washed him and replaced him in the cage". To this day, Gene has not confessed.

EVERYONE'S A CRITIC

During the Eighties, amateur rock group Blitzen were playing at the Grand Funk Lounge, near Newark, California.

Their set was not going particularly well and, after one rather long extended guitar solo, a loud booing sound began to come from the front row of the audience. Squinting against the glare of the spotlights, lead singer and guitarist Jakson Clifford – who had been responsible for the solo – sneered into the microphone: "I'd like to see you do better." The booing continued and so Jakson decided to set a challenge. "Come on up here then," he yelled, "and let's see you do better."

The audience went wild, but Jakson was rather at a loss for words when Eric Clapton strolled up on to the stage.

AN UNLIKELY STORY

In 1975, the imprisoned crew of a Japanese trawler were set free after it was discovered that they were speaking the truth. When they were found in the Sea of Japan clutching the remains of their ship, every single crew member told authorities that a cow falling from the sky had been the cause of the wreckage.

They were immediately arrested. They remained in prison until word of the case got out and Russian authorities admitted that the pilot of one of their cargo planes had stolen a cow from the edge of an airfield in Siberia, and put the creature on his plane before taking off.

However, when the cow began to get agitated, the crew pushed the animal out of the cargo hold. The animal fell 30,000 feet before landing on the trawler.

ON AIR DISCOVERY

A radio station in Minnesota ran a regular programme, where women could discover how much their men really loved them. The DJ would ring up the man, saying that they were ringing from a flower company, the man's business card had been picked and he had won a free bouquet of flowers to be sent to his loved one.

When Kim rang in to check on her man Greg, the DJ asked her whether she ever doubted Greg's love for her. Kim said she knew he was faithful, but wanted to give him a little boost into proposing marriage. However, when the DJ asked Greg who he wanted the card to be made out to, all the listeners were shocked to hear him say the name Anne. "Who's Anne?" asked the DJ. "My wife," replied Greg. Kim hung up after screaming expletives that led the radio station to issue an apology to listeners and remove the spot from the show.

Irvin Gazinski was awarded $1,750,000 after taking the Winnebago Company to court. Mr Gazinski had, some months earlier, been the proud owner of a new Winnebago motor home, and was driving along the freeway in California when he decided that he fancied a cup of coffee.

FOLLOWING INSTRUCTIONS

He put the vehicle in cruise control, and then left the driver's seat to get himself a drink. Obviously, the Winnebago then left the road, crashing and overturning on a grass embankment. Although uninjured, Mr Gazinski took Winnebago to court, suing them for not informing him that cruise control would not drive the vehicle for him. He was successful and was awarded over $1 million, as well as a new motor home. Winnebago also changed their instruction manual to prevent further court cases.

TEMPER TEMPER

When Pearl and Eric Wiseman teed off on their golfing holiday, they stopped their game briefly to watch a young man drive three successive balls into the water. In a fury, the man hurled his golf bag into the water after the balls.

The couple carried on their game, and were not too surprised to see the same man sheepishly returning to the water where he had thrown the bag. Curious, they watched as he rolled up his trousers, removed his shoes and socks and waded in.

To their amazement, he then unzipped the pocket of the bag and removed his car keys, then threw the bag – complete with expensive looking clubs – back into the water!

HAVING A BLAST

Joseph and Donna Fairbanks' mobile home in Little Rock, Arkansas was destroyed in 1999 after Joseph's attempts to check whether there was water inside a gasoline can went horribly wrong.

After shaking the can and peering inside, he discovered that there was not enough light and so used a cigarette lighter to look inside the can. This was when he discovered that there was flammable liquid inside the can, and the fumes immediately set light. Joseph then dropped the can on the floor, splashing the gasoline all around. Both he and Donna managed to escape, but their mobile home was lost in the fire.

BRINGING DOWN THE HOUSE

When two French delegates arrived in London in August 1976 for a trade meeting, they were warned that a big rival company might spy on them.

Therefore, upon arriving in their hotel room they set about searching for bugs or cameras.

They thought they had their suspicions confirmed when they found a bump under the rug in the centre of the room. It appeared to be a plastic dome covering some kind of metal pipe. Enjoying their role as detectives, the delegates set about removing the dome and pipe to find a large nut. After quite a struggle they unscrewed the nut and heard a large crash.

Unsure of what had happened, the delegates resumed their search for bugs until they were interrupted by the irate hotel manager, demanding to know why they had unscrewed the chandelier!

GUARD DOG

Man's best friend proved a life-saver for Australian couple Sandra and Martin Rossiter.

The couple returned to their Sydney home from an evening out to find their pet Dobermann – ironically named Tiny – choking to death in the lounge. Panicked, they took the creature to a vet friend of theirs who lived nearby. When examining Tiny, the vet made a gruesome discovery – the dog had been choking on a human finger!

Sandra and Martin telephoned the police and explained the situation. When the authorities searched the couple's house they found a glowering man, bleeding profusely from his hand. He had been hiding beneath the couple's bed armed with a knife.

DON'T **TRUST** ANYBODY

Jean Williams, of Croydon, England, was the victim of a rather unusual scam. She was doing her weekly supermarket shop when she noticed an old lady staring at her with tears in her eyes.

"Don't mind me, dear," said the old woman. "It's just that you remind me of my daughter. She passed away recently and I never got to say goodbye. I know it's an unusual request but it would make me so happy if you would say, 'goodbye mum' when I leave the supermarket."

Jean, a kind-hearted young woman, agrees to do this favour for the grieving woman. As she is at the checkout she sees the old lady leaving and shouts "goodbye, mum" to her, just as she promised. It is only when she sees her shopping bill that she begins to suspect something is wrong. The supermarket assistant explains to her that the old woman said that her daughter would cover the bill for her shopping as well as her own!

UNEXPECTED ADVICE

Jessica Anderson, from Seattle, Washington, had a lucky escape when help turned out to come from an unexpected place.

Driving home after an evening out with her friends, Jessica noticed a car coming up behind her. As it pulled alongside her, she was shocked to see the driver suddenly slow down, pull in dangerously close behind her and put his foglights on.

She sped up, but the car behind never left her alone, occasionally flashing its lights brightly. Shaking, Jessica pulled into her driveway, figuring that she had to make a run for the house. As she flew from the car, her pursuer pulled into her drive and yelled through his open window, "Call the police, call 911!"

It turned out that the driver behind, one Eric Price, had seen a silhouette of a man with a knife when he started driving past Jessica's car. When he had flashed his foglights, the man had ducked back down in the back seat. Every time the man had gone to stab Jessica, Eric Price had flashed his lights and saved her life.

A FAMIL-
IAR FACE

When 18-year-old Mary Allridge suspected that she might be pregnant, she decided to buy a pregnancy test from the local chemist.

The woman behind the counter glared at Mary with obvious disapproval as she made her purchase.

When she discovered the test was negative, she was relieved and began preparing herself for a dinner with her boyfriend's family, none of whom she had met before. The feeling of relief was short-lived, however, when she opened the door only to come face-to-face with the disapproving chemist, who turned out to be her boyfriend's mother!

PIECE OF CAKE

Retired Ruby Smith, from Canterbury, England, volunteered to bake a cake for a charity sale at her local church. She decided to bake an angel cake, but in her last minute rush she neglected to bake it correctly and the centre collapsed.

As there was no time to bake another, Mrs Smith used an empty toilet roll tube to prop up the middle of the cake. It looked perfect, and Mrs Smith arranged for her daughter Sandra to buy the cake so that no one would know. Sadly, her daughter was too late and Mrs Richardson bought the cake.

A couple of days later Mrs Smith was invited to a bridge afternoon at Mrs Richardson's house, where she was horrified to see her cake presented as dessert.

Mrs Smith started to say something, to explain before the cake was cut, but before she could say anything another lady commented on how lovely the cake looked. "Thank you," replied Mrs Richardson. "I baked it myself."

SHOP SHAPE

The owner of a large department store in London was making his annual inspection. As he entered the stock room he saw a young man leaning against a pile of unpacked boxes, whistling casually.

The store owner demanded that the man do some work, but the man remained where he was. Outraged, the store owner asked the man how much he made a week.
– "£300," the man replied.

– "Well," said the store owner, peeling off several notes from a roll in his pocket. "Here's a week's pay. Now get out – you're fired."

Returning to the shop floor, feeling rather pleased with himself, the store owner asked the manager who that young man had been. He was less pleased when he found out that he was a delivery driver employed by another company.

SHORT-CHANGED

A wannabe robber failed on his first attempt to steal from a Circle K convenience store in Louisiana back in 1995.

He walked into the store and placed a $20 bill on the counter in front of 20-year-old shop assistant Harry Jones, and asked for change. When Harry opened the till, the would-be robber pulled out a gun and demanded Harry place all the cash from the drawer into a brown bag and hand it over. Harry did as he was asked, and – after satisfying himself that the drawer was empty – the man ran out of the store, leaving the $20 bill and a very confused shop assistant behind. The till had contained only $14 and Harry was left unsure whether or not to report the 'crime' of being given $6 at gunpoint!

PICTURE THIS...

Joe Robertson had invited a few friends over to his new house for drinks, and to show off all the hard work he had done decorating the place.

The last room to be finished had been the downstairs toilet, and so Joe warned his guests not to use it, as the paint on the seat was still wet. Unfortunately, Amber Parry arrived late and missed the warning, so was rather surprised when she found herself unable to move from the toilet seat.

Swallowing her pride, she called out for help and – after much laughter – the toilet seat was unscrewed so she could stand up, however, they could not remove it from her skin. Joe telephoned a doctor friend of his, who came round as fast as he could.
– "Be honest, doctor," said Joe, "have you ever seen anything like this before?"
– "Well... yes," replied the doctor. "But I believe this is the first time I've ever seen one framed."

FAT CHANCE

Working as an attorney did not stop Phillip Shaefer, from Ashland, Ohio, filing this suit against Delta Airlines.

Mr Schaefer was flying with the company from New Orleans to Cincinnati. His complaint was that he was given a seat next to a fat man, and that – due to his neighbour's size – they were pressed up against each other for the entirety of the flight. Claiming that having to sit so close to this large gentleman for two hours caused him "embarrassment, severe discomfort, mental anguish and severe emotional distress", Schaefer then filed a suit against Delta for $9,500. The case is still pending.

MESSY MIX UP

Mark Murphy got away with a crime when his attempt to siphon petrol from Trevor Pearson's motor home went disgustingly wrong.

Instead of plugging his hose into the petrol tank, he instead stuck it in the motor home's sewage tank. His next step, as is practice when siphoning, was to put his mouth around the end of the hose and inhale deeply. When the police arrived they found Murphy, a very ill man, lying next to the motor home, with sewage all around him. Despite Murphy's attempt to steal from him, motor home owner Trevor Pearson declined to press charges, declaring the event "the best laugh I've ever had."

SUSPICIOUS MINDS

Larry Jump, a cement-truck driver from Dallas, Texas, was due to make a delivery around the corner from his own house, so he decided to drop in and surprise his wife.

However, he was shocked to see a shiny new Cadillac parked in his driveway. When he peered through the window he saw his wife having coffee with a handsome man in a sharp suit. Broken-hearted, Larry saw red and filled the Cadillac in the driveway with wet cement.

Upon seeing this, his wife ran out of the house and demanded to know why he was destroying the present she had just had delivered for him. The man having coffee with her was the car salesman.

COPY COMEDY

Warwick University student, Michael Menner, decided the only way to pass his course was to put one over on his professor.

When he was asked to write a marine biology essay, instead of doing the reading, Michael copied an essay written by another student years ago. The old essay included a detailed picture of a whale, and the student received an A grade. Michael did not have a lot of time, and so did not include the picture. When he received his paper back from the professor he was shocked to see that he only received a B grade, accompanied by the professor's comment, "I liked it better with the whale."

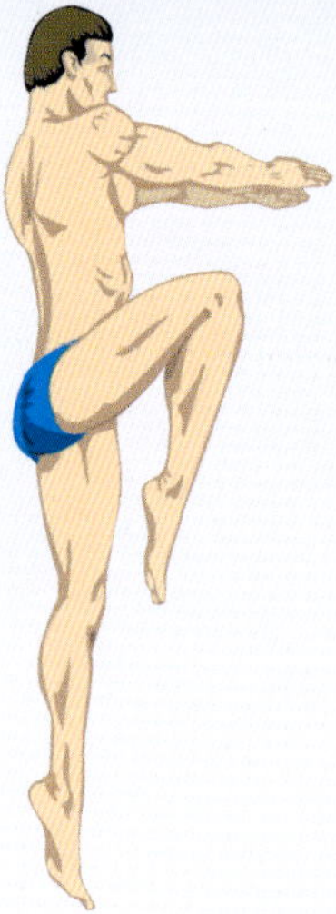

LUCKY BREAK

Australian high-board diver Shane Tate, was training for the Olympics and was given special pool privileges at the university he attended.

One night he was stood on the high board, preparing to dive, when he noticed the shadow he cast on the wall. In the half-light it looked as if his head was at an awkward angle, and his limbs were broken and twisted.

Shocked by this vision, he sat down for a second to recover himself. That was when the pool caretaker turned the lights on to reveal that the pool had been drained that day. Had Shane jumped, he would certainly have broken his neck.

UNDISCOVERED GENIUS

When late for a maths lecture, student Joe Scott saw what he assumed were that week's homework equations written on the blackboard.

He quickly noted them down and worked on them for a week before handing them back to the professor. After the professor has studied them for a week he calls the student to a meeting to discuss having his work published. It turns out the equations were not homework assignments, but examples of problems previously thought to be unsolveable that the professor had been using as examples in a lecture.

RUNNING ROBBERY

Out jogging one day, Matt Trevors was bumped by another jogger. Annoyed, Matt became enraged when he discovered that his wallet was missing.

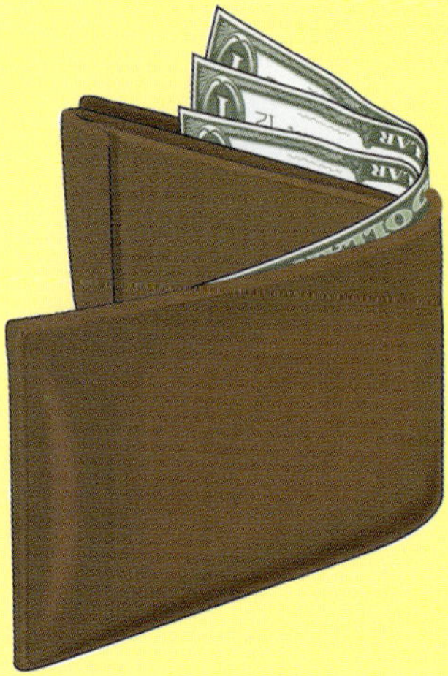

Determined not to take this, he took off after the other jogger. After catching up with him, Matt tackled him to the ground, yelling: "Give me the wallet!" Frightened, the thief complied and then took off.

Arriving home, Matt apologised to his wife for being late, assuring her that he had a good excuse. But before he can fill her in, she surprises him by replying, "I know – you left your wallet on the table".

ONE GOOD TURN

A terrifying experience one night showed Maria Drake never to judge on appearance.

Driving home late one night in Trenton, New Jersey, Maria heard on the news that a dangerous lunatic had escaped from the local asylum. The announcer warned that the man was not to be approached. Just then, Maria's car got a flat tyre.

Terrified, she got out and began changing the tyre as fast as she could, all the time looking around her. In her rush, she dropped the lugnuts needed to fit the spare tyre. She bent down to search for them, but they were nowhere.

Then she got the shock of her life as her search brought her face to face with a dishevelled looking man in a white asylum uniform.

Her heart in her throat, she gasped: "What am I going to do now?" and was more than a little surprised when the man replied: "Why not take a nut from each of the other wheels and put them on the spare?"

With shaking hands she did so, and drove safely home.

COMING UP TRUMPS

Michael Day was driving along the I75 freeway in Michigan back in the Eighties, when he saw a limousine at the side of the road. He pulls over and asks the limo driver if he would like any help, offering his mobile phone.

The driver accepts the phone, telling Michael that the car phone in the limo isn't working. After calling for help, the driver introduces Michael to the famous occupant of the limousine, none other than millionaire Donald Trump. Grateful for the assistance, Trump asks whether there is anything he can do for Michael. Feeling a little foolish, Michael asks Trump to send flowers to his wife, Doris, as he's sure she would really appreciate it. Sure enough, the next day a huge bunch of flowers turns up for Doris, but there is an even more pleasant surprise waiting inside the envelope. The card reads: "Doris, your husband is a wonderful man. I have paid off your mortgage – D. Trump."

TALK AIN'T CHEEP

When stuck for what to get his wife Ethel for her birthday, Jay Logan, from Orlando, Florida, decided that – as a bird lover – she would like a bird that could speak.

Not one to do things by half, Jay then went out and bought her a bird that spoke in eleven languages. This did not come cheap, and Jay paid out $100 for each language the bird spoke, plus an extra $100 for the creature itself. However, he thought it was worth it to make his wife happy.

Sure enough, when he got home from work, Ethel was there sporting a huge smile.
– "What did you think of that bird I sent you?" he asked.
– "Marvellous," she beamed. "It's in the oven now."
– "In the oven?" screamed Jay. "But that was a very expensive bird. It was meant as a pet. It speaks eleven languages."
– "Then why," asked Ethel, "didn't it say something?"

PATHETIC PAYOUT

Terence Dickinson broke into a four-bedroom American home – knowing the family were on holiday – and stole all their valuables. He decided to exit through the garage but as it had an automatic door, he was unable to get out this way. He turned to get back into the house, but the door had locked behind him and he was unable to break it down. For the remaining nine days that the family were away, Terence lived on Pepsi and dry dog food. Terence later sued, claiming undue mental anguish. Amazingly the jury agreed and ordered a pay out of half a million dollars.

As far as ridiculous court cases go, this has to be one of the best.

BEWARE OF KIND STRANGERS

Tim Latham came home in a foul mood and explained to his wife that, while shopping in the supermarket, he had noticed his keys were missing. When he got outside he realised his car was missing.

After informing the police they agreed to change the locks on their home the next day.

However, when they woke up the next morning, the car was back on the driveway, in perfect condition. The keys had been posted back through the door, along with a note.

The note read: "I apologize for stealing your keys and car, but I had an emergency that I cannot explain. Please find enclosed 4 tickets to see Arsenal play in the cup final this Saturday."

Being a big Arsenal fan, the man was overjoyed, and the next Saturday he took his wife and two sons to see the match. When they returned home, however, they discovered that they had been robbed!

The thief had deduced the man was an Arsenal supporter from his bumper sticker, and knew he would need four tickets after watching the house. He had discovered the address from the car registration in the glove compartment.

When Craig Tompkins saw a Porsche advertised in a local newspaper for £50 he assumed there had been a misprint, but decided to have a look at the car anyway.

ALL'S FAIR

The woman showed him the car and allowed him to take it for a test drive. It ran like a dream. He queried the price and was amazed when she confirmed that it was indeed £50. He handed over the cash and was given the relevant papers to sign, and the car keys.

With the sale confirmed, he could take it no longer and asked the woman why she was almost giving away such a valuable car.

"My husband has left me because he is having an affair with his secretary," she replied. "He left me a note saying the car and the house were his, and I was never getting my hands on them. He told me to sell them and send him the money. Would you like a house to go with that car?"

CUSTOMER SERVICE

When a rude passenger approached a gate agent at Heathrow airport he got more than he bargained for.

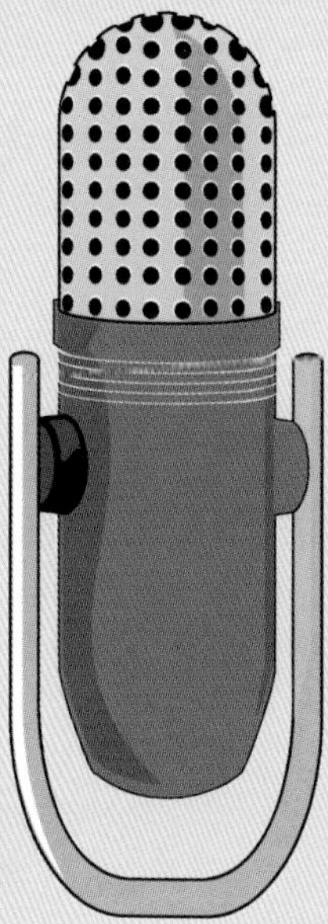

The man barged to the front of the queue and demanded to be served immediately. When informed he would have to wait, the man became angry and started yelling at the assistant, "Do you know who I am?"

Quick as a flash the assistant grabbed the PA microphone. "Can I have your attention please?" she said, her voice echoing round the airport. "We have a passenger here at Gate 17 who does not know who he is. Can anyone help?"

The passenger walked to the back of the queue red-faced while the people in line applauded the plucky assistant.

A FEW TOO MANY

Bob Smithson is driving home from a bar drunk when he sees flashing lights in his rear-view mirror. He pulls over and gets out of the car.

However, just before the police get a chance to breathalyse him, they are distracted by an accident a short distance along the road. As they run off, Bob decides to make his getaway and drives off.

The next day he wakes up with a massive hangover and the police banging on the door. "Sorry to bother you, sir," says one of the officers, "but we have reports that you were driving drunk last night."

Bob denies all knowledge and agrees when the police request to take a look at his car to check for any damages. However the smile quickly fades from his face when he opens his garage door to reveal the police car that pulled him over the previous evening!

QUIRKY QUESTIONING

Coroner George Wright was often called into court to explain details about the cause of death of an individual.

Over the course of several years, he built up a dislike of lawyers and some of the ridiculous questions they asked to try and catch him out. On one afternoon in 1997 this frustration reached a peak.

– "Before you performed the autopsy," said the lawyer, "did you check for a pulse?"

– "No," replied Wright.

– "Did you check for breathing?"

– "No."

– "Blood pressure?"

– "No."

– "So, it is possible that the patient was alive when you began the autopsy?"

– "No," replied Wright angrily.

– "Because his brain was sitting on my desk in a jar."

Unbelievably the lawyer continued: "But the patient could have still been alive nevertheless?"

– "Yes," sighed Wright. "I suppose it is possible that he could have been alive and practising law somewhere."

FLIGHT FRIGHT

A lifelong passion for aviation led Larry Walters to attempt something not recommended for those who want to live.

After his poor eyesight prevented him from being a pilot, he decided to build his own flying machine, by attaching 45 weather balloons to his lawnchair and filling the balloons with helium. He thought he would level off at about 30 feet, then shoot a few of the balloons with a pellet gun to slowly descend.

However, things did not go according to plan and, after his ties were severed, Walters found himself floating at 16,000 feet, where airline pilots were radioing news of his flight to their control towers. Scared to fire at the balloons in case he unbalanced himself, it took two hours before Walters worked up the nerve to fire the pellet gun. When he did he began to drift back down to earth, eventually becoming tangled in a power line, which blacked out a Long Beach neighbourhood for 30 minutes. He was then arrested.

WEDDING BLUES

The wedding of Kimberley and Charlie Parkins is certainly one that lives long in the memory of all those who attended. Everything was going well at the couple's ceremony in Elmhurst, New York. After the meal, the groom stood up to make his toast.

– "I have a lot of people to thank," he begins.
– "Firstly, thank you to you all for these wonderful gifts and for sharing this special day with us. Now I have a surprise for you, will you please all reach under your chairs."

When the guests follow his instructions they discover a photograph taped to the underside of each seat. There are gasps when they see a picture of the bride in a passionate embrace with the best man.

– "Finally," says Charlie, "I would like to thank my father-in-law for this $30,000 sit-down dinner."

With that he walked out and filed for an annulment.

NOT SO-SWEET REVENGE

Jacqueline Martin did not taken kindly to being dumped by her boyfriend Tad Jameson, and she was even more furious to discover that, just two months after they had separated, Jameson was getting married.

Martin decided to get revenge, and attended the wedding in Melbourne, Australia with a large bucket of wet cow dung. She had intended the dung for Jameson, however, changed her mind when she saw the beautiful young bride's sparkling white dress. After throwing the dung over the bride-to-be, Martin tried to make her escape, but was prevented from doing so by angry wedding guests, some of whom had been splattered with dung. Michael pleaded guilty to charges of assault in November 1997. On top of her three-year suspended sentence, she also had to reimburse the bride for her a $2,700 wedding dress and shoes.

UNEXPECTED ADVANTAGE

When Samuel Pitt applied for the job of bookkeeper in a brothel, back in the Twenties, he thought he had sunk pretty low. However, he discovered that, as he could not read or write, even the brothel would not employ him.

The woman who told him that he was unsuitable for the job did feel sorry for him, and gave him two shiny red apples to take away with him. When wandering the streets, Samuel managed to sell the apples to a stranger. He then bought more apples, and sold them at a profit. This success led, over time, to a grocery store, then a supermarket, then a chain of supermarkets, until Samuel Pitt was one of the wealthiest men in San Francisco. When asked by a journalist, "What do you suppose you would have become if you had learned to read and write?", Pitt replied: "I guess I would have been a bookkeeper in a brothel."

BUMPY TIMES

In June 1985, mother-to-be Julia Weinburg was browsing in a sports shop in Manchester, UK, looking for some sports equipment to help her regain her figure after the arrival of her baby, that was due any day.

She sensed someone was following her, but it was not until she attempted to leave the store that she felt a hand on her shoulder.

A security guard asked her to step back inside the shop, where he and the store manager took her to a back room and accused her of shoplifting a basketball.

Julia laughed at first, but became upset when she realised that they were serious. The only way of proving that she was not a thief was to show them her stomach, which she was about to do when her waters broke. This soon settled the matter, and nine hours later Julia gave birth to a son.

Passengers flying from San Francisco to Los Angeles were more than a little concerned when, on a refuelling stop, they saw their pilot wandering up and down the runway, wearing dark glasses and walking a guide dog.

FLYING BLIND

There was a stampede for the exit and several passengers demanded not only to change flights but to change airlines.

What had happened was, when going for his usual walk to stretch his legs while refuelling, the pilot had taken one of the passenger's guide dogs for a walk as a favour to the passenger.

Eventually the whole mess was cleared up, but not before the entire plane was evacuated and delayed by almost five hours.

NUMBER'S UP

The incredible plot of the Nicholas Cage movie 'It Could Happen To You' is based on actual events.

Phyllis Penzo was a waitress for 24 years at Sal's Pizzeria in Yonkers, New York. One of her regular customers was Robert Cunningham, a police officer. Usually a good tipper, Cunningham was short one afternoon, and proposed an unusual alternative. He asked Penzo to pick three lottery numbers and he would pick the rest. He then went to the newsagents across the street and bought the ticket.

The next day he presented Phyllis with a cheque for $3 million – half the $6 million jackpot he had scooped with their joint ticket.

SIGNING OFF

When Paul Ellis got back to his car, which he had left in a car park in Luton, UK, he was dismayed to notice that one side of the vehicle was badly scratched and dented.

Noticing a note tucked beneath the windscreen wipers, he breathed a sigh of relief, thinking that the culprit had left their details so he could claim on their insurance. However, what the note said was something very different. "Dear Driver, I have just run into your car and made a hell of a mess of it. As a crowd has gathered, I am forced to appear as writing you this note to apologise and to leave you my name and address. As you can see, however, I have not done so."

PICK-UP PUT-DOWN

Travelling salesman Ricky Roberts was getting sleepy on his long drive to Seattle, and so picked up a hitchhiker.

However, this was a move he soon regretted, as the man was rough-looking.

Feeling threatened, Roberts picked up another hitchhiker further along the way. This man was younger, and looked quite clean-cut. However, as soon as his car was on the highway, the young man pulled a gun from his pocket and told Roberts to pull over. He repeated the order, gesturing with the weapon.

The older hitchhiker took advantage of the gun being pointed towards the window and punched the younger man, knocking him out. The older man removed the pistol and the young man's wallet, explaining to Roberts that he was usually a thief himself, but he had decided to have a day off. Roberts never picked up hitchhikers again.

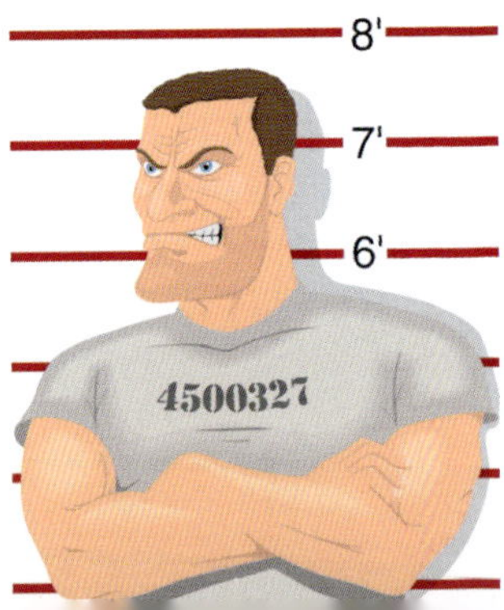

A mobile speed camera van in Canberra, Australia, was the victim of a rather spectacular practical joke playing by a gang of unnamed, as yet unidentified, youths.

CHASING THE CHASER

These teens stole the license plate from the van and placed it over their own. They then sped past the van containing the speed camera no less than 17 times. This resulted in the automated billing system sending 17 speeding tickets to a stationary van that somehow seemed to have caught itself on camera!

Harry and Charlotte Parker were the proud owners of a 22ft Bayliner boat and had travelled to Lake Isabella, California, to spend some time aboard their new purchase.

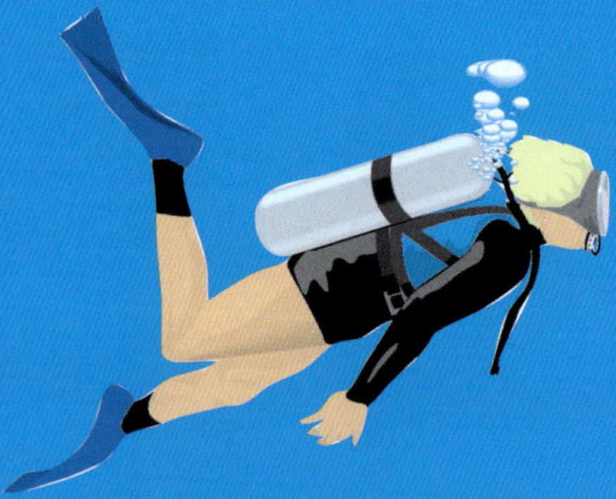

However, they were not having the success they had hoped for. New to boating, they were surprised that their boat seemed very slow and sluggish, despite everything appearing to be in perfect working order.

Convinced something was amiss, they pulled into a marina and asked for assistance. Everything above board was revealed to be running fine, so their helper, Brian, dived into the water to check underneath the boat.

When he surfaced, he was nearly choking because he was laughing so hard. Underneath the boat, still strapped in place, was their trailer.

SINKING FEELING

ON THE JOB

After working for a certain airline for a number of years, stewardess Kimberly Martin had had enough and handed in her resignation.

On her final flight she decided that she would liven up the usual preflight announcement, by phrasing it in the following way: "Ladies and gentlemen, welcome aboard. To operate your seatbelt, insert the metal tab in the buckle and pull tight. It works just like every other seatbelt, and if you don't know how to operate one, you probably shouldn't be out in public unsupervised. In the event of a sudden loss of cabin pressure, oxygen masks will descend from the ceiling. Stop screaming, grab the mask and pull it over your face. If you have a small child travelling with you, secure your mask before assisting with theirs. If you are travelling with two small children, decide now which one you prefer. Thank you and remember no one loves you or your money more than this airline."

PENNY FOR THEM

When Mike Hayes, from Rochelle, Illinois, was accepted at the University of Illinois, he was worried about how he would ever afford the tuition fees, until he had a brainwave.

He wrote to a Chicago Tribune columnist and asked him to ask all his readers to donate one penny each, reasoning that everyone could spare a penny. His scheme caught the columnist's and the public's imagination and soon Hayes was receiving donations from, among others, Miss America 1983, Debra Maffett.

Mike soon raised the $28,000 he needed, donating any extra to charity. His father, Bill, said later: "When Mike first told me the idea, I just laughed and said I thought it was dumb. Which shows you that he's smarter than I am."

IN-FLIGHT ENTERTAINMENT

Back in the Fifties, when people were still wary about air travel, one airline ran a promotion allowing the wives of businessmen to accompany their husbands for free, so that they could see for themselves how safe flying was and put their minds at rest.

It was a success, and the names of both husbands and wives were logged on to a system so that, later, the company could write to the women with a questionnaire about how they had enjoyed their flight. However, the plan backfired slightly when the response from more than half the women was "What flight?" Many divorces followed.

GRRREAT MATE

When the following advertisement ran in an Edinburgh local newspaper, there were over 600 responses...

"SBF (single black female) seeks male companionship. Age, ethnicity unimportant. I'm a young, svelte, good-looking girl who loves to play. I love long walks in the woods, hunting, camping and fishing trips. Candlelight meals will have me eating out of your hand. Rub me the right way and watch me respond. I'll be at the front door when you get home from work wearing just what nature gave me. Call the number and ask for Daisy." When callers rang, they were put through to a local dogs' home. Daisy was a Black Labrador. Not only did she find a loving owner, but Daisy also proved that man's best friend really is a dog.

ARRESTING SENSE OF HUMOUR

In Alberta, Canada, police regularly check stalled vehicles on the highway whenever the temperature drops to single digits and the snowstorms come. On one such check, Constable Bill Wisen came across a car stuck in deep snow on the side of the road, with its engine still running.

Inside was a man, passed out with a vodka bottle on the seat next to him. The man awoke when Wisen tapped on the window and, resigned himself to the fact that he was caught, the man then pushed down the accelerator. The speedometer needle began to rise and the drunkard thought he must be moving, but the car was well and truly stuck.

However Wisen, having a sense of humour, began to run on the spot next to the car. As the speedometer got higher, showing 20mph, then 30, then 40, Wisen kept jogging in the same place. He then yelled at the man to pull over. Totally flummoxed, the driver did so and was arrested. He then wondered aloud all the way to the station, how the policeman had run at over 50mph to pull him over.

Staying at an expensive hotel in Alabama, Troy Richards was very annoyed when he woke up in the morning covered in insect bites.

NOT SO EXCLUSIVE

As he had to rush to catch a plane, he had no time to complain to the manager, but instead sent an angry letter, complaining about the cleanliness of such a pricey hotel. He received a lovely letter in response, apologising profusely, saying that this had never happened before and that they had no idea what had gone wrong, but they were looking into it. This would have satisfied Richards if his own letter had not been included in the reply, complete with a Post-It attached that read: "Another miserable customer. Send standard insect apology letter. No refund."

CALLING A BLUFF

George Phillips of Meridan, Mississippi, was startled when he looked out into his back garden and noticed there were some people in his garden shed, stealing his equipment.

Quickly he rang the police. They asked if anyone was in his house, and when he replied there was not, they told him that there were no patrols available and that he should lock the door and wait for someone.

Not prepared to watch his valuable equipment go walking, George waited only 30 seconds before ringing the police again.
– "Hello," he said. "I just called you about some people in my shed. Well, don't worry, because I just shot them all."

Within five minutes three police cars, an armed response unit and an ambulance turned up at George's house. Of course, the police caught the burglars red-handed.
– "I thought you said you'd shot them," said the police officer.
– "I thought you said there was no one available!" retaliated George.

FOOD FOR THOUGHT

A criminal career was the wrong choice for 18-year-old Frances Jamison, who walked away empty-handed after his attempt to hold up a fast food restaurant in Ypsilanti, Michigan, went slightly awry. After entering the establishment at 8.50am, Jamison pulled out a gun and demanded that the server open the till and give him the cash.

Bravely – as he was faced with a weapon – the server replied that he could not obey Jamison's demand, as the till would not open without a food order being placed. After a brief moment's thought and a look at how much change he had in his pocket, Jamison ordered onion rings. The server informed him that onion rings weren't available at breakfast time. As Jamison did not have enough money for the breakfast menu, the sorry would-be criminal slunk out of the restaurant.

A VERY SURPRISE PARTY

A young woman and her fiancé were left rather red in the face after an evening of romance went horribly wrong.

Mary Steenburg and Todd Faber decided to have an evening alone together to celebrate Mary's 21st birthday. As they both still lived with their parents, Mary's mother and father agreed to go out for the evening to give the young couple some privacy.

One thing led swiftly to another, and soon Mary and Todd were both in a state of undress. At this moment, Mary's mother telephoned the house and asked her daughter to switch the washing machine off in the basement. Todd, wearing just his underwear, scooped up the equally undressed Mary in his arms and whisked her down the basement steps. They were about halfway down when all the lights went on and relatives of all ages jumped out from their hiding places yelling: "Surprise!"

"It certainly was a surprise," said Mary later, "but I'm not sure who was shocked the most!"

Clive Yates, from Dorset, UK, placed a complaint with the Trading Standards Commission after seeing an advert for an 0891 number, with the tagline "Hear me moan".

FALSE ADVERTISING

Rather than reading the rest of the advertisement, he picked up and dialled, expecting to listen to a sexy woman's voice. When he heard a tape of a woman nagging her husband for not doing the household chores, he listened for the entire length of the 10-minute tape before hanging up.

The tape was a jokey promotional gag, and this was clearly pointed out on the advertisement. Consumer watchdog, the Trading Standards Commission, refused to look into the complaint, saying that Yates: "Got what he deserved".

KILL OR CURE

When Yvonne Darnley's turn came to man the desk at the Poison Control Centre, in Leeds, UK, she received a call from a very upset woman. The woman had found her infant daughter eating ants and had become hysterical with worry.

After checking a description of the ants to confirm they were not poisonous, Yvonne told the woman not to worry, ants were not harmful and there was certainly no need to take her daughter to the hospital.

There was a moment's silence before the woman asked: "So there was no need for me to give her ant poison to kill the ants then?"

SURGICAL ERROR

When Michelle Knepper's plastic surgery went wrong, she sued her doctor, Timothy Brown. Doctor Brown was Board Certified, but only in dermatology, not in plastic surgery. Knepper, from Vancouver, Washington, found Doctor Brown in the phone book and went to him twice for liposuction, once in 1997 and again the following year.

The doctor agreed that his advertisement – which said he was Board Certified, but was not specific – was false advertising and paid a settlement to Knepper. However, this was not enough for Knepper, who also sued the publishers of the phone book for carrying the advert. She won damages of $1.2 million in her case, and her husband Jeff was awarded $375,000 for "loss of spousal services and companionship".